POETRY SHE WROTE II: REFLECTIONS OF THE HEART

BY DEE FREEMAN

Bloomington, IN authorHOUSE® Milton Keynes, UK

AuthorHouse™
1663 Liberty Drive, Suite 200
Bloomington, IN 47403
www.authorhouse.com
Phone: 1-800-839-8640

AuthorHouse™ UK Ltd.
500 Avebury Boulevard
Central Milton Keynes, MK9 2BE
www.authorhouse.co.uk
Phone: 08001974150

© 2006 DEE FREEMAN. All rights reserved.

No part of this book may be reproduced, stored in a retrieval system, or transmitted by any means without the written permission of the author.

First published by AuthorHouse 12/7/2006

ISBN: 978-1-4259-6693-5 (sc)

Printed in the United States of America
Bloomington, Indiana

This book is printed on acid-free paper.

Photo of beautiful Hawaiian sunset
taken by
Myron Freeman, Sr.

ACKNOWLEDGMENT

I am immensely grateful to my family and friends who helped provide me with the patience, inspiration, love, confidence and space to compile and write this book: my husband, Myron, my biggest supporter and constant friend-whom I simply adore for reminding me over the years that I can do this; my beloved son, Frederick, has fueled my heart-I'm happy to have shared so many beautiful experiences with him; our daughter, Janeece, has blessed our hearts with her sweet, sweet spirit-making us proud; our son, Myron Jr., has given us years of happiness, helping us to become stronger in our faith; my special-not so little anymore- Giovanni (peanut), the love of my life, has given me more joy in his fourteen years than anyone should ever have; my grandson, Mario, a lovable little man in his own right, has warmed my heart; third grandson, little Myron #3, rejuvenates my heart and tests my energy whenever nearby; my siblings, my entire family, my close and not so close friends, all who encourage and continue to support me.

Thanks, I love all of you. May you find awareness and contentment in your search for your own true meaning of life and may these words give you the needed encouragement to become the best 'you' ever.

POETRY SHE WROTE II: REFLECTIONS OF THE HEART

TABLE OF CONTENTS

FOREWORD... xi

ASPIRATIONS 1

    WANTING TODAY..3

    ONLY, IF I COULD!! 5

    SOMETIMES 7

    SEIZE THE MOMENT 9

    I NEVER TIRE 11

    YOU, MAKE A DIFFERENCE 13

    WEAVING A TAPESTRY 15

    WISHING AND HOPING AND PRAYING........17

SEARCHING 19

    SEARCHING..21

    WHO AM I ?..23

    INCREASE IN ME...25

    FOR WHAT EVER REASON 27

    LOOKING FOR SANITY 29

    SO AS I THINKETH 31

    SPEAK TO MY HEART, LORD.......................33

    SELF AWAKENING 35

    A CHALLENGE FOR US!! 37

  MY SOURCE 39

PASSION 41

  ALLEGIANCE TO HUMANITY 43
  FERTILIZED 45
  GIVING MY BEST: MY GIFT 47
  MY LIFE'S PASSION: 49
  THE FLOW: CIRCLE OF LIFE 51
  QUIET, MY PASSIONATE SOUL 53
  AT THE DOOR I KNOCK 55

HEART REALITY 57

  THE NATURAL WOMAN IN ME 59
  AIN'T I SOMEBODY TOO? 61
  REFLECTIONS 63
  BEAUTY OF IT ALL 65
  MY HEART REALITY 67
  SOLID IN THE SKIN I'M IN 69
  I BELIEVE 73
  STILL ME 75
  SELF PORTRAIT 77
  TODAY, I DREAM A WORLD 79

REAL LOVE 81

  FROM ME TO YOU 83
  WEEPING STREAMS 85
  LOVE: IN THE FLESH 87
  LIMITLESS LOVE 89
  TOUCHING LIVES 91

    WITHOUT LOVE: UNACCEPTABLE 93
    LEAVING A LEGACY 95

CLOSING STAGES 97
    ALTERED 99
    ONLY BREATHING 101
    LIFE SENTENCE 103
    I WILL LIVE, UNTIL 105
    IF I MUST 107
    FLEETING SUBSISTENCE 109
    VISIONS 111
    TOMORROW 113

EPILOGUE 115
AFFIRMATIONS 119
ABOUT BOOK 131
OTHER BOOKS 135
ABOUT AUTHOR 137

FOREWORD

The optimism in Dee Freeman's third volume of poetry is just as contagious as it was in her first volume, Oceans of Love: To Us From Us. Freeman's poetry reveals in the author a profound faith in God on the one hand, while querying the reality of human despair. From the opening epigraph from Herman Hesse's *Reflections,* which stresses the oneness of all living beings, to the self-eulogy that ends Part II of *Poetry She Wrote*, Freeman traverses a plethora of emotions from yearning in sections titled "Aspirations" and "Searching," to resolution in sections titled "Heart Reality" and "Closing Stages." Poems like "You Make a Difference," share the didacticism of nineteenth century poet, Frances Ellen Watkins Harper. Others, such as "Fleeting subsistence," are more abstract and ambiguous.

Freeman's own generous spirit is evident in poems like "Only, If I Could." The speaker is a mother expressing to her child all that she would do for him if she only could. The final stanza reads

> If I can do for you things simply and great
> And make life stupendously good
> I will not stall, stammer, or hesitate
> I'll do it for you my child, only, if I could.

The poem is a mother's meditation on all the ways that she would protect her child from the hard realities of life, directing him toward love and away from self-destruction.

Other poems, like "Ain't I Somebody, Too?" address the realities of living with social and economic disadvantages that serve as barriers to self-actualization. The questioning voice in the poems of the "Realities" section offer a contrast to the optimism of the opening sections of Freeman's collection. And, it is the startlingly clear and well-developed sense of VOICE that is most apparent throughout the volume, regardless of whether a given poem's speaker is engaged in the aforementioned didacticism in poems such as "Seize the Moment," assuming a more innocent, questioning stance like the speaker in "Ain't I Somebody, Too?" or "Who Am I?," or simply and calmly reflecting on metaphysical matters in the beautiful "Sometimes."

In the poem "I Never Tire," Freeman seems to invoke Zora Neale Hurston's "How it feels to be Colored Me" with a twist, for she uses her poem to point more overtly to the absurdity of race-based discrimination.

It is fitting that Freeman includes a section titled "Passion" in this collection. Desire overwhelms that section, but it is a narrowly directed desire to be of service, to be part of the solution, to come to the end of life knowing that one has lived a generous and loving life. The self-eulogy that ends Part II ends with the following words:

> Look upon me
> Today
> Hold my memory
> Forever
> Take heed and prepare
> As I am
> Today
> So shall you be
> Tomorrow

Many of the poems in Parts II through V of *Poetry She Wrote* are decidedly religious in theme, reflecting the writer's strong religious convictions. I have known Dee Freeman for most of my adult life, and I always knew that she possessed tremendous spiritual beauty. I am glad that she decided to share that beauty with the world in such a beautifully organic manner.

Lovalerie King, PhD;
Assistant Professor of African American Literature,
Penn State University.

"We must become so alone, so utterly alone, that we withdraw into our innermost self. It is a way of bitter suffering. But then our solitude is overcome, we are no longer alone, for we find that our innermost self is the spirit, that it is God, the indivisible... for in our innermost soul we know ourselves to be one with all being."

-Hermann Hesse, Reflections, 195 ed.
Volker Michels, 1974

ASPIRATIONS

"Who shoots at the mid-day sun, though he be so sure he shall never hit the mark, yet as sure as he is, he shall shoot higher than he who aims at a bush."

-Sir Phillip Sidney

Wanting Today

Only, If I Could

Sometimes

Seize The Moment

I Never Tire

You, Make A Difference

Weaving A Tapestry

Wishing And Hoping And Praying

WANTING TODAY

I want to- leave this world better
        because I passed this way
I want to - give happiness to someone
        every single day

I want to - be kind to all I meet, expressing
        love with a tender smile
I want to - give to all the best I have
        by going that extra mile

I want to - leave this world nicer
        because I was here
I want to - comfort and aide someone
        who's in need of love and cheer

I want to - leave the world less lonely
        because I showed I care
I want to - always be available to help
        anytime, anyplace, anywhere

I want to - give God the praise for answering
        my humble and meager prayer
I want to - look to Him for all my needs
        for I know He's always there

I want to - share a Blessing with someone
        who is less fortunate than I
I want to - show the world I'm God's child
        As His grace lifts my wings to fly!

I want this - today and every day!

Dee Freeman

"I'd give you the world if it were mine to give
    I'd give you advice on how to live
I'd give you the sun and every ray it shines
    This I'd do son, because you are mine."

                Dee Freeman
                Poet, Author, Speaker, Literary Advocate,
                      Producer, Host., Jan 2004

ONLY, IF I COULD!!

If I can share the love I have to give
      I'll give it ever so freely
If I can advise you the best way to live
      I won't hesitate to offer it-
Hopefully discreetly.

If I can turn each choice you've had to make
      Into the right decision that is perhaps a test for you
If I can guide each footstep you must take
      I'd place them solidly, wherever is best for you.

If I can do these things, and it's in my might
      To handle life's difficulties for you instead
I would do them now to make your life right
      For the future that lies ahead.

If I can go through the agony you have felt
      Or absorb your pain and your sorrow
If I can change the raw deals you've been dealt
      And give you a happy and bright tomorrow

If I can just tell you and you will understand
      That you can avoid the mistakes made by another
That you can be sensitive, when being a strong man,
      These are facts, not just words from me
Your mother.

If I can do all the things I mentioned above
      Solve your problems for you instead
I would if I could, just to show you my love
      That will follow during the years ahead.

If there is a way I can set you free
      From any hang-ups or any inhibitions

Dee Freeman

I'm willing to partition God with my strongest plea
      For your welfare and your safe protection.

I know it isn't easy to be understanding and strong
      Or courageous in these world conditions
If I can change for you all the things that are wrong
      I will do it now, with no thought or hesitations.

If I can do for you things simply and great
      And make life stupendously good
I will not stall, stammer, nor hesitate
      I'll do it for you my child, only, if I could.

SOMETIMES

SOMETIMES, I DREAM:
I envision worthwhile contributions I made,
where I make a difference

SOMETIMES, I MOURN:
I dwell at the bottom of my soul's
unbridled consciousness

SOMETIMES, I CRY:
I feel despair when I see the condition
this world is in now

SOMETIMES, I ACHE:
I long to help this world, anyway I can,
anyway, just somehow

SOMETIMES, I PRAY:
God then lifts my spirits
and they're held aloft by His Grace.

ALWAYS
I lift my eyes to Glory
And with my uplifted heart, see,
God is truly in this place.

"Seize the very first opportunity to act on every resolution you make, and on every emotional prompting you may experience in the direction of the habits you aspire to gain."

-William James

SEIZE THE MOMENT

Seize the moment, don't procrastinate or
waste your time away.
Realize now, you'll grow old, then actually waste away
yourself some day.

Be productive, doing something that helps you enjoy life, make
progress, and grow:
read, write, sing, or paint - these things may be of great benefit.
Hey, you never know!!

The time you now waste is forever gone. It'll never come
back to you.
Believe me, you'll regret your lack of action later in life, when
there is little to do.

Time has a way of moving on; even when it's not the way you
would choose.
If you don't take advantage of the chances you've been given:
oops, too late! Sorry ! You lose!

Get up! Get busy!! Seize the moment – don't waste another
precious hour.
Make haste now - if you don't use them, you'll lose your talents
and God given power.

Don't be one who looks back on memories and say "you know, I
should have done a few daring things".
These are melancholy memories and you don't
need the sadness they can bring.

So don't procrastinate. Seize the moment; don't waste portions of
your existence away.
This gift of life is something to cherish. I as you should,
use it wisely-to its' fullest-every single day.

Dee Freeman

"When younger, I sheltered my feelings often,
Because I didn't want to be hurt.
Now, older and wiser;
I recognize and appreciate my own self-worth."

Dee Freeman
Poet, Author, Speaker, Literary Advocate,
Producer, Host., Oct., 2005

I NEVER TIRE

I never tire of my ethnicity
    The fact I am black
I simply tire of being treated inhumanely
    Where the deck is always stacked

I never tire of my blackness or my
    Quest for knowing the real me
I simply tire of being demeaned
    As my stolen heritage
Hampers my understanding of my identity

I never tire of my search for humanity
    My desire to be treated with respect and dignity
I simply tire of others' connotations that prevent
    Me being the me I am meant to be

Dee Freeman

"Keep your life simple. Decide what is important and what is unimportant and do not waste yourself on unimportant issues. Save your thoughts and energies and put both to use on the things that count."

-Rhoda Lachar

YOU, MAKE A DIFFERENCE

You are what you choose to be…
You must also be
The change which you wish to see.
For You too can make a difference

Make contributions-   not confusion
Make happiness-   not sadness
Make decisions-   not excuses
Make smiles-   not frowns
For decisions are what make the world go round

Make motivation-   not procrastination
Make praise-   not criticism
Make peace-   not war
Give love away, isn't that what it's for?

Make positives-   not negatives
Make tolerance-   not impatience
Make haste-   not waste
You and I can make a difference

Make excellence-   not mediocre
Make improvements-   not stagnation
Make confidence-   not doubt
Excellence should be what we're all about

Make hope-   not hopelessness
Make integrity-   not indecency
Make progress-   not regression
The time is now, we must strive toward perfection

Dee Freeman

Make wealth- not poverty
Make I can- not I can't
Make love- not hate
Yes, We can make a difference

Make commitment- not disagreement
Make helpful- not hurtful
Make courage- not fear
These are **some** reasons God has placed us here

Make I will- not I won't
Make I do- not I don't
Make **right now** not—- maybe someday
Make I will - for there is always a way

Make a listener- not a gossiper
Make reassurance- not worry
Make **a friend** not an enemy
Yes, You and I **can** and will make a difference

Make gratitude- not bad attitude
Make impact- not impasse
Most of all,
Make a pact to assert love and faith
For only they will last

WEAVING A TAPESTRY

Weave me into the caring mother
    Valuing my children each joyful day
Not as much for happiness I attain
    As the happiness I give away

Weave me into a wife
    Taking to heart vows uttered
In innocence, love and truth
    Not that I'm so brave
But in the fact my love is pure
    And lasts since times of my youth

Weave me into the daughter
    Respecting a mother's
Warm and gentle love
    Not so much depending
As sharing a loving relationship
    As destined by our Father above

Weave me into a sister sharing
    Heritage and strong familial pride
Not so much in selfish achievements
    But in conjunction with ancestral
Strength as I've always tried

Weave me into the person
    Achieving prosperity and wealth
As lives and connections begin
    Not so much in personal gratification
As in sharing cherished memories
    With dear and treasured friends

Weave me into the embroidered tapestry
    Without malice, hatred or sin
Weave me into the warm and shielding tapestry
    Your loving hands intend

Dee Freeman

Along with wishing, hoping and praying
Comes the need for action to bring to fruition
All your wishes
All your hopes
All your prayerful desires

    Dee Freeman
    Poet, Author, Speaker, Literary Advocate,
    Producer, Host, 10/05

WISHING AND HOPING AND PRAYING

I'm wishing and hoping and praying:

Wishing, I could do more to help my people
And myself

Hoping, we will eventually find equality
That's our birthright

Wanting, to emotionally evolved to see more clearly
What it really means to be black
Or to be free

Hating, how we are always demeaned…
Just because

Praying, deep down within
       We'll grow
       We'll overcome
       We'll be better for the struggle
       We'll succeed

Through all my desires, dreams, wishes, hopes and prayers
I'm yet, confident to be the insde me
Proud to be the outside me and
Proud of the person…the reflection of me I see

My wishing and hoping and praying…pays off!

SEARCHING

"Before we can realize who we really are, we must become conscious of the fact that the person we think we are, here and now, is at best an impostor and a stranger."

>Thomas Merton,
>The New Man, 74, 1961

Searching

Who Am I?

Increase In Me

For What Ever Reason

Looking For Sanity

So As I Thinketh

Speak To My Heart, Lord

Self Awakening

A Challenge For Us!!

My Source

SEARCHING

My essence:
              S!   to the highest Starlit galaxy
        R
     A
   O
S

R O C K E T S!   across a thousand Milky Ways

D
  I
    V
      E
        S!   to the deepest depth of every ocean
                  Every sea

S A T R
  C T E S   across the wide expanse of
                  Mountains in search…

In search of my authentic self

Searching, here and there
Searching, everywhere

Only to return; spent, breathless…
Finding a mere reflection of
Uncertainty in the mirror
Hanging right here
Across from me

"Make it thy business to know thyself, which is the most difficult lesson in the world."

-Miguel de Cervantes

WHO AM I ?

Jesse Jackson tells me "I am somebody"
Michael Jackson sings "I'm the one in the Mirror"
Maya Angelou says I'm a
"Phenomenally Phenomenal Woman"

Yet I despair
Is it because I yet hear the voices of the
former slave owners saying
I am diminished…not a full citizen?

Aretha Franklin bellows
I should demand "Respect"
The Staple Singers vocalize
"Respect yourself"
Helen Baylor melodically croons
"I've got the Victory" and I agree

So why do I despair?
Why am I despondent; lowering my head?
Is it because
I can't find my right place in society?

My friends say, girl, you're gifted and talented
My husband tells me I'm his beauty queen
My history & heritage bequeath
I'm a descendant of Kings and Queens

Yet, my doubts flourish;
Surface and rob me of realizing
And appreciating my self worth

Martin Luther King, Jr. shouts from the mountain top
I'm "free at last"
Stokely Carrmicheal and Malcolm X proclaim
I now have and have always had "Black Power"
James Brown bellows I should

"Say it loud, I'm Black and I'm Proud"
The Holy Word gently reminds me
I am a child of the King

So, I look in the mirror
Ponder, delve deep within myself
There I see activity
I see the birth of a New ME!
A brand New ME

Now I See Who I Am
Now I can sing!
Now I can shout to the world!

Now I can stand tall
Yell it from the mountain tops!
Now I can walk Proudly; with my head held high
Now I know "I AM SOMEBODY"!

That reflection in the mirror is ME!
I, AM ME!
And "I Gotta be me"
I am an intelligent creation of the Almighty
I am a PROUD African-American!
I am a PROUD WOMAN!
A proud sistah!

Who has found self Love
The awesome power of Black Love
Opens like a cocoon
And awakens my spirit

It transforms me
Into the real me
I truly long to be
Creating my true identity

INCREASE IN ME

Increase in me as never before
    Help me Lord, to love you even more
Increase within me the spirit galore
    Through You, it augments my loving store

Increase in me your still quite peace
    Which I need to make my will decrease
Allowing my obstinacy to entirely cease

Increase in me your will
    The solitude to be still
The abundance to be filled

Increase in my soul
    The resolve to be bold
Also the spirit to be whole

Increase in me, though not for show
    The ability to increasingly grow
The attitude, love, and wisdom to know

Increase in me a lowly unworthy human
    Your knowledge to quietly understand
Through life's trials I need to hold to your unchanging hand
    Your love and increase will allow me to ultimately stand

Dee Freeman

"Always dream and shoot higher than you know you can do. Don't bother just to be better than your contemporaries or predecessors. Try to be better than yourself."

-William Faulkner

FOR WHAT EVER REASON

For what ever reason
    I was awakened to a new day
For what ever reason
    I've been given this poem to say

For what ever reason
    I was spared, yet not my neighbor
For what ever reason
    He's seen fit to leave me here for

For what ever reason
    He allows me to courageously stay here
For what ever reason
    I'm blinded and cannot even see clear

For what ever reason
    I can't know, yet I search to know His will
For what ever reason
    He permits His will which I may fulfill

For what ever reason
    I pray He has plans for me to see tomorrow
I've paid for yesterday today; and from my future
    I've plans to borrow

So, though I can't fathom why
    I deserve to live for yet another season
I'm happy and blessed He's spared my life
    I thank Him for what ever reason

"No man is free who is not a master of himself"

-Epictetus

LOOKING FOR SANITY

Trying to locate from whence life itself comes,
I travel within the depths of my being and reflect
How has creation dealt such a mighty punch to
Even yet, bewilder life's origin and destiny?

I seek to loose the bindings of my meager soul…to squelch
The flames of inner emotions-singeing desires
Though I sink deeper, d e e p e r
Peering into darkness
Longing for light to spring from gloom
Simultaneously, I rise from my abysmal depths
Rise…rising h i g h e r

Even here in solitude, my essence slumbers
Concealing diminishing, retreating sanity
My flaming desire erupts again and again
Intimate and utter solitude can no longer hold me
Captive within my self

My skin may enslave my muscles and bones
My brain may enslave my mind
Yet desires effortlessly erupt…
Bursting forth-as blood rushes to
Heal a wounded heart-
Frantically seeking to find
Within my depth
The force which will enlighten
Will tenderly touch and awaken
Will open up a renewed awareness…

Thus, compassionately aroused
Still, desparately searching and
Yet, lovingly transformed
I find peaceful…
I find meaningful…
I find anticipated…
SANITY!!!

Dee Freeman

"Public opinion is a weak tyrant compared with our own private opinion. What a man thinks of himself, that is it which determines, or rather indicates, his fate."

-Henry David Thoreau

SO AS I THINKETH

A magical eruption of the nerve
Impulses in my brain create the
Thoughts I think, I think.

I think, therefore I am.
What I think I am,
I am...I think.

And what is it that I think I am?
I'm not convinced that what
I think is truly thought.
Maybe what I'm thinking is only
An impression I've been taught.

Maybe I'm camouflaged as beliefs
Tossed to and fro.
Maybe I'm me, not real
But me incognito.

Often I think I'll never truly know
What my outward appearance seem to show.
I'll never understand enough
To conclude that I truly exist;
Exist in the here and now...
I think I do, at least I wish.

The mind, the consciousness
The soul, the self
The thought, the feeling
The complete essence, and all else;
I ask my thoughts,
From whence do they all come?
What is the entirety, the whole and total of
All the above sum?

Dee Freeman

What heavenly realm has spewed
Forth the breath that I inhale;
That travels the waves of my consciousness
Before I then exhale?
What gives rise to this
Concept of contemplation;
Ultimately altering the mind
And manipulating it's deliberation?

Thus, this upsurge opens
An awareness that rises from my depth
To enlighten mind and psyche;
Allowing all thoughts to ponder on
Only the me I know
I am to be.

SPEAK TO MY HEART, LORD

The essence of my prayer to You each imminent day
Gives me power to on this journey –diligently stay
As You speak to my heart Lord
Your grace and mercy sculpts:
My sad heart…glad
My poor heart…wealthy
My bitter heart…sweet
My scared heart…courageous
My weak heart…strong
My ill heart… healthier
My cold heart…balmy
My childish heart…wise
My blind heart…sightful
My hurt heart…healed
My hungry heart…filled
My run down heart…uplifted
My little heart…big
My loveless heart…loved
Speak to my heart, Lord
Speak to my heart
I pray…
Just one word from You will
Bless my entire day…
So, please speak to my heart Lord,
For only You know what to say!

Dee Freeman

"My search for life's big mystery has led me to the realization of each small daily mystery."

                        Dee Freeman
            Poet, Author, Speaker, Literary Advocate,
                  Producer, host., 11/2005

SELF AWAKENING

I feel anguish - I hurt, why?
Why do I always feel so?
What is it that makes me
Ache like this?
I ask, for I truly want to know.

I observe… just outside my window
The playful
Birds chirping with glee.
Yet me, I ache with a dull pain
And sadly envy the rain,
For even it is happy.
It sounds of laughter
Merrily chuckling
It's way down an outside drain.

It has a mission…to bring about
Renewal and birth
Teaming with the sun, they
Reach into the depths of
Mother Earth

There to continue natures deeds;
Their yearly ritual to awaken the seeds.

Envy overwhelms me
I too need an awakening…
I'm screaming, it's vividly clear
Inside and out loud, to no avail
For no voice can I hear.

My screams fall onto deaf ears or
Maybe no sound materializes.
Do my soundless pleas go
Totally unheard? Never crystallizing?
I beg…
Please rain down, saturate me.
Wash away this lunacy,
This uncanny uncertainty.

Dee Freeman

I linger here between
Sanity and regret,
Allowing the beaming sunlight
To sear my outer shell, and yet,
Sanity repels even the sun's charring singe,
Not allowing hushed whispers of my mind
To penetrate consciousness of anykind.

Only my breath is permitted
Access to my inner being.
Isolation is real, I think.
Only my essence loiters
In this room of bleakness,
As I slowly sink.

My spirit bids my unburied life to return;
Return from desolation.
Return to a real
Place of melancholy isolation.

Arise!...Open up...Awaken!
Swell up into wholeness.
Defy any urge to fade
Into despair and nothingness.

Let love soar again,
Opening up to let the soul stir.
Let this brain-a mass
Of active synapses-meta-morph...
Awakened from this blur.

Clean out and release the cobwebs
That entangle and bind;
Open up, awaken, now transformed mind.

Awaken renewed body;
Awaken high-spirited soul;
Awaken brave self to a place
Of self love and become totally whole.

A CHALLENGE FOR US!!

The challenge is to:
Raise our awareness, raise our expectation
Keep our demands in the forefront of the Nation

Break free from the shackles of all type prejudice
Regenerate and rejuvenate a bold stance for equal justice

Close the ever widening economic gap
Break free from the stigmatized social trap

Stress the issues of complete national equality
Remove the stigmas of cultural inferiority

Think out of the "box"…find our loud voice
Create some prosperous strategy, with unlimited choice

Gather our voices and energize our political clout
Lets get on the move…simply put, get the lead out

Stop the slow moral and social declines
Upgrade and energize the stagnant minds

Loosen our minds from the harsh psychological constraints
Find real truth, for reality may sometimes appear what it ain't

Educate the masses, learn of and treasure our history
Take control of our destiny and heal our scarred dignity

Elevate our selves from the mire of the bottomless pit
Wake up and unite…get up and get on with it

Rise from intellectual abuse
Stop the dying from excess drug misuse

Bolster self-esteem and show self love
Ask for guidance and power from above

Light a heated fire under your seat and mine
Let's get up and get cracking, for it is **certainly** about time!!!

Dee Freeman

"Think of God more often than you breathe."

-Epictetus (A.D. 55?-135?)
Fragment, 119, tr.

George Long, 1890?

MY SOURCE

From the dawning of time
When the world came into being
Like a sudden and powerful blast spreading forth
Reaching wide…
Mystery loomed over human existence

On the horizon of forever
Hovers the answer to the trivial
Questions of humanity:
> Who are we?
> How did we get here?
> Why are we as we are?
> What is life about?
> Why is there such suffering?
> What awaits at the end of life?

We feeble bits of flesh and bone
Maturation of clay…dust of the earth
Seek desperately to understand the
Source of our existence…
Which is far beyond our frail comprehension and grasp

This shrouded mystery exceeds my imagination
Evades my limited perception
For the source of my being is
Awesome
Absolute
Unfathomable

I spend a lifetime-a mere flash in the span of time
Seeking to feel His presence
And wanting to have a relationship
With the Divine

Dee Freeman

Wanting to know Him
To be in His presence...
My nearness and zeal somehow authenticate
His compassion

I wrestle with my comprehension
For I know He is close... I feel Him,
Yet He's incomprehensible – too complex in His nature
I dare not extend beyond myself-
My own meager understanding

His complexity exceeds simple consciousness
I do not find Him in the mighty rushing winds
He alludes me while riding the thunderous storms
He's evasive in the tumultuous earthquakes
Neither do I see Him in the ferocious fire

I'll never see or touch Him, yet I seek Him
He knows my desperation
He watches, He waits, He listens
Then-in His time-He touches me
In the stillness, the calm, the quite of my soul
I feel Him, I hear Him...the still quite voice
Speaks to my heart

He reveals Himself only to my
Innermost self, for words are inadequate
Then I am with Him and He with me

I cannot conceive His Holiness
I cannot understand His plan for my destiny
I cannot define His Divine presence
I only understand I am His
Then, I know...He is:
    My Strength
    My Redeemer
    My Life
    My Source

PASSION

"Without passion man is a mere latent force and possibility, like the flint which awaits the shock of the iron before it can give forth its spark."

                Henri Frederic Amiel,
                Swiss philosopher

Allegiance To Humanity

Fertilized

Giving My Best: My Gift

My Life's Passion

The Flow: Circle Of Life

Quiet, My Passionate Soul

At The Door I Knock

ALLEGIANCE TO HUMANITY

My desire is to
Spur on spectacular thoughts
Energize them to positive activity;
I want to
Help stimulate an intuitive mind
And reach into the core of it's creativity;

My dream is to
Contribute to the improvement of knowledge
So it is absorbed by all throughout;
I yearn to
Offer comfort and wisdom to one
Who knows little of what life's all about;

My goal is to
Have a positive impact on little ones
Who are in much need of care;
I hope to
Be an advocate for improvement of all
Especially those exposed to despair;

My plan is to
Do anything to alleviate pain
Sorrow, anger or discontent;
Then, I feel
I am doing the things
Through His Goodness…which were meant.

"Trust yourself. Create the kind of self that you will be happy to live with all your life. Make the most of yourself by fanning the tiny, inner sparks of possibility into the flames of achievement."

-Foster C. McClellan

FERTILIZED

I want to be like the fertilizer within good soil.
I want to be that foundation a youthful and fresh seed
Falls upon and eventually absorbs.

I want to be the sustenance, the nurturer,
Who will provide needed nutrients
Enabling a young embryo to not
Only take root, but thrive and sprout heartily:

>Growing, budding, developing,

>Emerging, evolving and becoming better-

>In every way.

I want to be an agent of productive change.
I want to be a fertile base that somehow aids in the
Transformation…rising from nothing, from noone,
From nowhere…
To develop into something, someone,
Somewhere…
Becoming fruitful, bountiful;
Able to command an abundant future-
Unsurpassed
By anything or
Anyone…
Anywhere.

Dee Freeman

"I long to accomplish a great and noble task, but it is my chief duty to accomplish humble tasks as though they were great and noble."

-Helen Keller

GIVING MY BEST: M Y GIFT

What can I give, be it great or small? I wonder to
      myself, what is it I have to offer someone?
Will writing these few verses of motivation
      be of benefit in times yet to come?

I certainly don't have huge sums of money to build
      or donate magnificent dwellings.
I do have warmth, love and ideas
      of self sufficiency, of which I'm now telling.

I haven't external wealth, or megabucks, nor can
      I make a hefty payment of gold.
I simply offer words of strength to produce internal
      wealth enriching the essence of the soul.

I can't give back to my community many riches,
      or frivolous material things.
I can share with you heartfelt wisdom;
      this, from the depths of my soul doth spring.

I trust these messages of inspiration I give, will encourage
      someone to be the best he/she can be.
This exchange of gifts will have a stamp of
      approval of how the Almighty uses me.

Giving reaps sevenfold, so give your best and watch
      the handsome return; believe-the best is yet to come!

"We are shaped and fashioned by what we love."

-Goethe

MY LIFE'S PASSION:

<u>Energize</u> positive activity of not only my heirs
Forth coming, but my peers who may suffer empty
Hollowness

<u>Stimulate</u> intuitiveness that produces exceptional
Creativity, igniting sparks of flaming ingenuity

<u>Intensify</u> wisdom so it oozes and spurts from
Every pore of every soul

<u>Kindle</u> love and comfort via kindness, so its
Radiant beam shines bright as the North Star

<u>Accelerate</u> hope, wellbeing, and
Self improvement to generate a productive future

<u>Alleviate</u> pain, sorrow, anger and discontent
Uplifting our souls to blossom and soar

<u>Provide</u> understanding amid challenges
So those, with whom I interact, will ultimately know
Self and Truth

Passion shapes and motivates!
Come on! grab some with me and lets' navigate life to new heights!

"High aim forms high characters, and great abjectives bring out great minds."

-Tryon Edwards

THE FLOW: CIRCLE OF LIFE

the blood of my ancestors oozed and spewed
        at the crack of the master's whip
leaving their bodies limp, lifeless at times
        as did the journey in the hull of a slaving ship

the spewed blood flowed, enriched and fertilized
        the soil upon which it did spill
giving rich life, sustenance and pride…giving
        gusto to heirs growing richer still

the pulsating rhythm of this blood rushes
        continually channeling memories left of my distant past
this flow keeps ancestral royalty in the veins of a culture
        struggling through ages ago, yet still destined to last

our survival depends upon our use of today and tomorrow
        and mostly utilization of lessons learned
let this flowing circle of life throb—-pumping determination
        into eager minds and deserved lives we've painfully earned

Dee Freeman

I will lift my mighty pen
Put it to paper…
Inscribe the story
etched in my head;
engraved in my mind;
carved on my heart
and flowing from my fingertips!!!

                              Dee Freeman
                              Poet, Author, Speaker, Literary Advocate,
                                    Producer, Host., June/2006

QUIET, MY PASSIONATE SOUL

D
    O
        W
            N   Deep

    Submerged within my soul's depth
    Sits a quiet passion
    Utterly silent, uttering no sound;
    Not even a whisper.

At rest. Motionless. Tranquil. A stillness so calm that
Even I know not that it exists.

Sleep… Sleep my quiet passion,
Until you reach that right moment…
Until touched gently;
      Until Aroused and quietly awakened.
      The passion then stirs, ever so slightly.
      Suddenly kindled to gentle movement,
      Like swaying with the rhythm of a Ballerina
      Smo-o-othly flowing, it glides yet higher.

                    up.
              up,
Now, rising,   up,

Now in perpetual motion. Continuously stirring. Swiftly.
Exhilarating. Electrifying. Igniting.
Now exploding with the brilliance of Haley's Comet.
All aglow! Moving. Rising ever higher!

Now on fire!!…on fire!!

Passion of my soul, take flight!!

W R I T E !!

When I seek, You show me
When I ask, You answer
When I knock, You open the door for me

Though I am not worthy of all You do for me,
I knock and You are always there for me.

> Dee Freeman
> Poet, Author, Speaker, Literary Advocate,
> Producer, Host., Oct., 2005

AT THE DOOR I KNOCK

Lord, at the times of my deepest
    And most dire despair
At the door I knock
    And You show up there

When I'm confronted with burdens
    I alone cannot bear
At the door I knock
    And again You're right there

I realize, as I exhaust all humanly efforts
    To become a person…thoughtful and meek
That only through Your benevolence
    Will I attain what I seek

So to gain audience
    As one of Your blessed flock
In awe and reverence Lord
    I stand at the door and knock!

HEART REALITY

"The end of art is to figure the hidden meaning of things and not their appearance; for in this profound truth lies their true reality."

Aristotle, Greek philosopher

The Natural Woman In Me

Ain't I Somebody Too?

Reflections

Beauty Of It All

My Heart Reality

Solid In The Skin I'm In

I Believe

Still Me

Self Portrait

Today, I Dream A World

THE NATURAL WOMAN IN ME

The woman in me:
>Naturally wants to do everything, all the time,
>For everyone - Only if I could

The woman in me:
>Naturally wants to give all of me, all the time, to everyone,
>Wondering, if I really should

The woman in me:
>Naturally wants to be all I can be,
>Then be even more and more
>She wants to share all my love, endlessly, thinking
>Isn't that really what love is for?

The woman in me:
>Naturally is all wise, all caring, all willing, and all knowing
>With all my virtue, empathy, patience, insight and
>synergistic energy flowing

The woman in me:
>Naturally sows the seed bringing about continuous
>procreation

The woman in me:
>Giving birth to a child, giving birth to a people,
>Giving birth to an entire nation

The woman in me:
>Naturally is all mankind; from whence the whole
>Universe sprung

The woman in me:
>Naturally is all humanity, smartly packaged into one

The woman in me:
Naturally *is* me:

"Your inner connection to
    Your Omnipotent creator is
        What makes you 'who' and
            'What' you are"

Dee Freeman, Poet, Author, Speaker, Literary Advocate,
                    Producer, Host., Oct., 2005

AIN'T I SOMEBODY TOO?

SAY, What'cha thinking? Can you tell me?
    What thoughts are running through your mind?
I can surmise from the look on your face,
    Whatever you're thinking ain't very kind.

Just hold on, think about life and creation,
    God made me just like He made you,
So why you think you're better than me?
    What? Ain't I Somebody Too?

Your look is conveying dislike.
    Are you thinking I should not be here?
Your glare, frown, and the shake of your head
    Awaken in me a once dreadful fear.

You always belittle me with cruel words,
    Speaking them without giving much thought.
Saying how things should still now be,
    As when I was sold and bought

Take a minute now, and look at yourself,
    Who the hell gave all power on earth to just you?
I was placed here as well and will no longer be denied.
    What'cha thinking now-huh, Ain't I somebody too?

Hey, let's look at things from my perspective
    The constitution says, yeap, I am totally equal to you.
Just give me my inalienable rights, here and now!
    For, I know, I am and have always been — Somebody Too!!

"To reflect is to receive truth immediately from God without any medium. That is living faith...You are as one who has a private door that leads him to the King's chamber..."

        Ralph Waldo Emerson (1803-1882).
        Journal, 29 July 1831

REFLECTIONS

I enjoy solitude
I like to be alone to ponder
To think quietly or maybe
Even meditate
To me, these are refreshing and calming
They put my mind in a gentle
And tranquil state

It is then, in the calm, I feel relaxed…
Overtaken by a peaceful
And consoling rest
I know deep within
I'm connected to an Awesome power
Loved and truly blessed

I don't have to solicit advice about this
I recognize it for myself
I know where He's brought me from
Better than anyone else

I sit, thinking deeply
In solitude, thanking Him divinely
For being my guiding light
When situations burden me down
As my best friend
He quickly makes them right

I ask Him to watch over me
Advise, aide…always protect me
I know
He'll forever be here
When all other friends leave or reject me.

Dee Freeman

It's at these precious moments of reflections…
I feel Him closest beside me
He calmly without fuss or bother
Lets me know He's here to guide me

I humble myself and
Again thank Him
For all He's done for me
He allows me safety and security
As His love and peace comforts me

I love my times of solitude…
Peaceful moments of refelection
With my heavenly Father
He gently welcomes me
Each time we meet
Letting me know - to Him
I'm never a bother

BEAUTY OF IT ALL

Life is a beautiful mystery.
Understanding this
Mystery is
An eternal quest of all.
Yet no one has ever
Unearthed an inkling of awareness.

We search…looking into
The very depth of our souls,
Our being.
Searching inside and outside,
Looking for every hidden clue…
Even the slightest trace
Pointing to understanding.

Destiny, however,
Moves us along like the breeze
Catching the bellows of a kite.
Sometimes pushing,
Sometimes pulling,
Always soaring high,
Dipping only
Occasionally,

Pausing,
Awaiting another strong gust of sanity…
Wistful imagination;
Insight that will
Propel us to heights
Where we feel
We can touch
The face of God.

Thoughts sometimes levitate in
A state of unconsciousness,
Hoping there the answer lies.

Dee Freeman

We long to realize oneness with nature
Hoping this union will provide
The key to the puzzle

Over and over,
Fate showers us with surprises…
Like a sudden April downpour
Rolling in on the soft clouds
Cooling the earth and then

Dissipating as suddenly as it appeared
With sometimes little evidence
It was ever there-
A flash in the mind's eye
Did it really happen?

We may never solve the enigma
It looms on and on
 "What will be, will be."

We also seldom grasp
Or appreciate the mystical bridge
Between living and dying –

Between the death of one soul
And the birth of another.
One reaching out,
Consenting to a connection
Within a higher realm of existence; the other
Finally succumbing.

The unsurpassed, magnificent
Beauty of it all
Evolves each single time
The womb opens-
Expelling a
Beautiful new mystery.

MY HEART REALITY

My authenticity opens the language of my heart;
Paints magical words in my mind;
Awakens a comprehension
Residing in my brain…
I then, value the wonderment
And recognize my reality of life is:

An Adventure, I dare to live;
A Beauty, I unveil, behold and delight in;
A Challenge, I rush forward to meet;
A Duty, I execute well;
An Expression, I articulate eloquently;
A Flower, I savor the smell and inhale its' beauty;
A Goal/game/and gift, I press forward to
      Achieve/play and accept;
A Hill, I easily climb;
Imagination, I use as inspiration to
      Bring reality into view;
A Journey of daily strolls,
      Allowing bits of wisdom to permeate;
Knowledge saturating my being,
      Emersing me fully;
Love, given freely whenever and where ever I can;
A Mystery, I'm destined to unfurl, unfold, and undo;
The Nature or nurturing of all there is;
An Opportunity, I use to propel action;
A Puzzle, I work to solve;
A Quest, I'm destined to conquer;
Respect, I value and hold in high esteem;
A Song, I sing; a Struggle, I'll fight;
A Tragedy, which may periodically surface;
Unselfishness, cultivating a sharing attitude;
Victorious, as I strive to become a winner;
Wisdom, I seek, once found I spread;
An X-rated movie, I fight to upgrade for all to see;
Yen and Yang, both needed for vital balance;
Zealous zeal; an emotion I couple with passion for eternity-loving it all.

"Nature…endowed us with pride to spare us the pain of knowing our imperfections"

> La Rochefoucauld (1613-1680).
>
> Maxims, 36, 1665,
> tr. Louis Kronenberger, 1959

SOLID IN THE SKIN I'M IN

Although I'm always physically
emotionally
and spiritually making and remaking myself
and relentlessly trying to connect
to redefine
even redesign this elusive inner self
I'm proud to be who I am -
Proud to be here
Proud to be me
At this point in destiny

Some times I feel
my entire consciousness
seeks the world's acceptance of who I am
the me I've become
Why should I care
or desire such acceptance
I ponder?
What's hidden deep in my
unconscious self?
Unrest? I wonder!

Does my psyche somehow reveal
me diminished
because it has not yet elevated
beyond the Willie Lynch theory
playing with my head
keeping me thus forever
confined?
Enslaved? Nearly dead?

Then
at that lowest point
a power surges
erupts, gushes
outpours and ultimately overspills
as my will to triumph
over such a mind set
keeps me ever motivated to be
the best me yet

I therefore
emerge
aided by my
Omnipotent God
I emerge
from deep obscurity
I emerge
summoning my true inner might
to deal with being real in
this the skin I'm in

Nevertheless, storms rage periodically
I often labor
to quiet the tempest
seething within
I look for the fuse of inspiration
to ignite
thereby vanquishing any other
smoldering disturbance in sight

Searching
probing
penetrating deep inside
in solitude
I grasp sustenance that
has been molded
sculptured
embedded
into my being and it
it alone creates what could be
what should be
from what is

So, even though
I sometimes descend
into a seemingly bottomless pit
I wonder
speculate
and question what's going on
within and without
I never demean myself nor ever doubt

I simply meditate on my reality
feeling secure
to be in
this the skin I'm in

Still, keeping
the outer me radiant, youthful
healthy and appealing
there are times I put forth great efforts
just to love me as
I am,
my whole body
my authentic self
my total person
my entire being
me, myself and I

This same me, with
my mind, my consciousness
my soul
my spirit
my divine force
my essence
and my core
all share this space

So we
The Trinity and me
sharing this space
this time and this place
are proud to be genuine
firm and solid in this
"the skin I'm in."

"The belief that becomes truth for me…is that which allows me the best use of my strength, the best means of putting my virtues into action."

> Andre' Gide (1869-1951). *The Counterfeiters*, 2.4, 1925, tr. Dorothy Bussy, 1951

I BELIEVE

There must be a reason why we exist
I delve inside to find an answer to this

What is my mission, my soul's purpose here on earth?
What am I destined to do from the day of my birth?
Am I to go out and spread the Father's Holy word?
Am I to teach the gospel until it is finally heard?

What's the intention in His Holy will?
What's the mission I'm here to fulfill?
What's the purpose of His divine and timeless plan?
Where in His righteous will do I humbly stand?

In response
Something inside tugs and pulls so strong
Something unseen keeps me moving right along
I know, many things that happen are out of my control
However, He gives me a faith onto which I must hold

I believe we've been given a start so now's the time to begin
I believe we've been befriended so we may now be a friend

I believe we have life, so we may live
I believe we've been given, so we may give
I believe we have been touched by His Holiness
I believe we have been blessed so we may bless
I believe we've been given help so we can lend a helping hand
I believe we've been nourished by His word so we're able to Stand
I believe we've been seekers who sought out His willI
I believe we've been healed for His will to be fulfilled

These are things I believe we are put on this earth to do
I'm striving to walk in His footsteps, emulating Him…
How about you?

Dee Freeman

"Keep true, never be ashamed of doing right; decide on what you think is right, and stick to it."

-George Eliot

STILL ME

Me! I'm still that little kinky haired girl
    The one who knew nothing about the world
The one who thought her Negroid features
    Were ugly and made her appear like some
Scary creature—roaming the dark in only dreams.

Me! I'm still that little caramel pixie
    Born in the south, near the heart of Dixie
The one who never liked the size of her lips
    The one who pinned her nose with close pin clips
Trying to make it smaller, or so it would seem.

Me! I'm still that little solemn, slow talking child
    The one who kept all feelings inside or low and mild
The one who cried silently, thinking no one else cared
    The one who never spoke out, because she was
Way too scared—of what the world would say to
    Dampen her starry, yet shielded beam.

Me! The brand new me!! Now the me I see; the possessor of
    Bold yet lovely features—the kind many yearn for, and
The caramel colored hue many others burn for.

Me! Now the me I see; have the desired sized
    Plump luscious lips—without having to buy them.
The soft, smooth supple type, and someone's always wanting
    To try them.

Me! Now the me I see; speaks out loudly,
    No longer intimidated, but speaking boldly what's
On my mind. Now, knowing that my ancestor is the
    Mother of all mankind.

Still Me! The woman I am now, pleases the shadowy
    Pixie of the past and smiles for Blessed I am!
As, now the me I see; truly cares for me,
    This older version of the little kinky haired, caramel colored,
Slow talking, mild mannered pixie; directly from Dixie.

I see myself clearly, through the eyes
That stare back at me
Yes, this reflection I paint is mine

Each day I must
Clean the mirror of life
So my image is not smeared
But always sparkle and shine

>Dee Freeman,
>>Poet, Author, Speaker, Literary Advocate,
>>>Producer, Host, Oct., 2005

SELF PORTRAIT

As the years swiftly pass by
    And I find more years behind me than ahead
As my once dark thick hair has thinned
    And drained to silver upon my head

I will still dream and reminisce on
    Exciting times I once had
Prompting me to exhibit a portrait unfinished
    That without touchups could make me sad

I've welded brushes of life-sometimes dripping full
    Sometimes empty-to the naked canvas of my soul
I observe a need to erase traits of sorrow and bitterness
    Touching them up with wisdom to make a masterpiece whole

This self portrait of life I continue to paint
    With soft colors of every hew
Hoping to cover smears of bitter regret, yet uncover
    Happy yesteryears with brightness streaking through

When the picture is finished, the brilliant hews of life
    Dim and slowly fade from view
I want my self portrait to emit a radiant
    Love and legacy spilling warm over the edges
Of my heart
Driping
Spreading all over
From me to you

Dee Freeman

See yourself as you wish to be;
Dream a you, that you only wish to see.
Life is decidedly what you yourself make;
Dream it, then become that dream and more-
When you awake!!

Dee Freeman
Poet, Author, Speaker, Literary Advocate,
Producer, Host, Oct., 2005

TODAY, I DREAM A WORLD

Today, I dream a loving world
Today, I create the world I dream
Today, I see a loving world
Today, I be that loving world I dream
Within and without
As I continue to dream

Today, I rise up
Sharing
Uplifting
Not rejecting, but
Caring
Helping
Even protecting

Today, I open my world
Extending to you
This world I dream

Today, come dream a world with me
Today, come see what I see
Today, come create the dream with me

Today, be what I be…
A better world
A loving world
A world of harmony
For all humanity
The world I dream today…
A world of peace, love and unity

REAL LOVE

"Two consistant motions act the soul.
And one regards Itself, and one the Whole.
Thus God and Nature link'd the gen'ral frame,
And bade Self-love and Social be the same."

Alexander Pope,
An Essay on Man, 3.315, 1734

From Me To You

Weeping Streams

Love: In The Flesh

Limitless Love

Touching Lives

Without Love: Unacceptable

Leaving A Legacy

FROM ME TO YOU

DEAR ONE,

If you would please, take a minute, as this message is for you. You may not have a burning desire to know my thoughts on life, but just indulge me. I find it heartwarming to reminisce on memories and with your permission, I'll express my hopes and desires for your future. Did you know, I think you're great and I'm happy to have known you for so many years. I am pleased we've shared wonderful experiences and precious time together.

I cannot insist you do anything at this particular moment, nor listen, for that matter, even though much of what I suggest in my following words, could be of benefit to you. You alone must live your life. I cannot live life for you, nor can I live my life through you. I do however, pray you'll take positive actions, without delay, because tomorrow is never promised to anyone.

As humans, we have our weak moments. Those moments when we've strayed from our predestined paths. In fact, I've been very slow-possibly suffering from low self-esteem myself-to embark on a successful path. From the voice of experience, I therefore, encourage you to start now, put procrastination in your past. It is however, never too late to become the best you possible; the time can never be better than now .

I hope I can say something here to inspire, motivate and spur you on to become the best you - ever. To aid you in your quest, these are some must do things: read, study, seek wisdom, broaden your horizon, and by any mean necessary, absorb all the knowledge you can. Knowledge is the key that opens up the world and its riches to you.

An easy and simple way to become wise; practice listening to those with layered experiences, who also wish to share them.
Put into use the positive advise given by elders, educators, ministers, and community leaders. Often, even your parents may well have some helpful words of wisdom. Yes, parents may occasionally go off the deep-end, but we do have your best interest at heart. We are also your number one (#1) supporters-on most days and in most ways. I personally wish I had used more of the advice my mother gave me. In retrospect, the lady turned out to be pretty smart, indeed.

LISTEN! LEARN! UTILIZE! We all can learn valuable lessons from others if we'd just listen. We can often benefit from their advice when we use it objectively. We won't use all we've been told. We must digest and utilize what is advantageous and of course, discard what we regard as useless.

Our human nature is: to help others; to encourage the young; and assist in making this a better world. I'm confident you realize this and have many ideals and goals in place for yourself, while traveling this long, winding journey through life. So, God's speed to you.

I am hopeful you will always succeed.

> SO FROM ME TO YOU - I GIVE YOU LOVE
> FROM ME TO YOU - I GIVE THIS ADVICE
> FOR (thru the ALMIGHTY) IT WAS
> FROM ME TO YOU
> THAT "I" GAVE YOU LIFE.
>
> From me to you son,
> Your mother

WEEPING STREAMS

I wept streams for that junky
Trying to get his high on
I wept cause, he's not caring that the bed he now lie on
Could certainly be the bed he die on
He buy it   Then try it
Now rely on it   Soon die on it

I wept rivers for the sistah walking the streets
I wept cause, she trying to find a few tricks
So she can get a real fix,
Not realizing she at risks
With those trying only to get their kicks.
She don't respect it   Won't protect it
They compel it   So she sell it

I wept oceans for that young man
Who now sit behind bars
I wept cause, he gotta
Repay his debt to the stars
And stripes for taking a few jars
From the shelves—-maybe a pack of cigars,
Hoping to turn his scars into stars
To improve a life before the bars
He stole them   Then sold them
Now sitting,   Behind bars that hold him

I wept streams for that mother
Who now has to be on welfare
I wept cause, she live in a place that don't even care
How she and her children fare
No, it ain't fare that no one else care
Who will help them out of this despair?
Each day she repeat-same ole, same ole
Then, she can't sleep
So she also weep

Dee Freeman

Can you now… understand how… I wept oceans,
Rivers, streams
For those who lost their dreams
I wept streams, or so it seems
Let's you and me wipe and dry every weeping eye
Do more than just sit idly by
Generate some bright sunbeams
Create some mo'e dreams
Be about action, cause we can do this… as a team
We just gotta damn up the causes of all these weeping streams

LOVE: IN THE FLESH

She's up before the sun
Undaunted by the pile of tossed
And misplaced curls...some matted
Some dangling
Standing stalwartly looking to the heavens

Daybreak...without fail she braves the newness
She looks back, her mind unfolds the unforgotten
Grief, heartache, suffering
Soon past times become
Clouded by dim visions of the future

She looks ahead, then searches
Her heart for signs of renewal
Of revival
Her faith, her belief, her fortitude
Are all likened to that of an
Old oak tree, standing
Unshaken'd by the storm

Her precious heart
Pure courage and
Layered experiences
Seem to swell, smooth and soothe the soul
Mending all broken fragments of existence

Giving of herself so completely
She, the keeper of our seed
Vessel of life
Somehow commands will
Commands the very essence of breath
Life ... destiny

She hurls rows upon rows of loving supplications
Which like a spiraling pyramid, ascend
Each floating upward...skyward
Meeting in heaven where every single one
Blends with another to form one of her
Loving prayers for her own...humanity

Dee Freeman

"To wait an hour—is long—
If love be just beyond—
To wait eternity—is short—
If love reward the end—

> Emily Dickinson (1830-1886).
> "To wait an hour—is long"
>
>
> (complete poem), 1863?

LIMITLESS LOVE

Perfect love:
        No boundaries…..Bursting through all confines
        Endless…..   No beginning, no end
        Timeless…   Past, present, future, always

Transcends spirit….   The soul
Reaches beyond flesh… The grave
Soars above galaxies…. The heavens

Pulls on the strings of my heart

Makes music
        Melodic….. Symphonic burst
        Showering us at every juncture of time
        Before, after, never, always, endlessly

Reaches beyond beyond - Unconditionally

No boundaries - No limitations

Limitless love…Flowing from above

Then to you…from me

Dee Freeman

Reach out; gently touch someone:

With your words-say it

With your actions-do it

With your heart-feel it

With your love-share it

Dee Freeman
Poet, Author, Speaker, Literary Advocate,
Producer, Host, October, 2005

TOUCHING LIVES

You often touch lives:
As evidenced here-many are:
Touched by Your presence
Given hope by Your prayers
Supported by Your kindness
Warmed by Your touch
Encouraged by Your faith
Strengthened by Your love
Uplifted by Your compassion

Many are touched by Your presence-Lord
You're always here to:
Lend an ear
Share a moment
Whisper an encouraging word
Lend a helping hand
Bless with supplication
Surround with love
Heal with assurance…
You touch lives often
Use me as Your vessel Lord, to touch more

"That love is all there is,
Is all we know of Love."

        Emily Dickinson (1830-1886).
        "That Love is all there is."
        undated

WITHOUT LOVE: UNACCEPTABLE

Even with the attainment of the highest degree of academia;
the success and status of the rocket scientist;
the spirituality of the Pope, himself;
without pure faultless love and respect for self and others,
you are less than a speck of sand
washed away by the evening tide
to be lost forever-sinking
to the bottom of the ocean.

Even with the wealth of riches untold;
an acquired ability to solve the unsolvable mystery;
the ability of a genius mind;
without pure faultless love and respect for self and others,
you are less than the fleck of residue of mud
that has been trodden under foot
then, swept from the floor as dust to drift
with the breeze, forever.

Love, will determine our deliverance.
With love and respect in our heart;
the improvement of humanity on our mind;
our eye on the prize;
God on our side;
we can be,
we will be,
we are,
a child of the King
and worthy.

With love, we are true conquerors and fully
Accepted by God.

Dee Freeman

To you, my heir,
I leave my legacy;

For you, my heir,
I desire the best;

From you, my heir,
I accept nothing less

For you are my legacy-make me proud!

Dee Freeman,
Poet, Author,
Producer, Host,
Literary Advocate
Oct., 2005

LEAVING A LEGACY

Leaving a legacy of morality-
Not an effortless piece of cake-
Requires dedication and sacrifice
For in this game… high is the stake
Filling every waking moment with the desires
To become knowledgeable and wise
Raising self esteem and self awareness
To eliminate cloaks of subtle disguise
Living above the haughty taughty stuff
Not indulging in the cocky mammy fluff
A legacy I wish to leave-

Recommending fair play, sportsmanship
Patriotism and financial advice
Offering wisdom to create a happy
Safe existence to predictably suffice
Instilling a sense of pride to be the best of who you are
Teaching every trait of creativity
To manifest an intense desire to go far
Scribing your name and mine into memories
Of future generations
Actively engaging off springs to secure
The survival of our nation
A legacy I desire-

Like the villages of ago
I wish my legacy to show
Encouraging respect for elders and in general
Respect for all of mankind
Producing attitudes of self love and survival

Dee Freeman

So no one is purposely left behind
Leaving a legacy of goodwill
To a world I wish to uplift
Leaving a legacy to improve this world
Is my endowment and my gift

I have being, thus my heir…
You become my greatest legacy

CLOSING STAGES

Confucius said, "We don't know yet about life, how can we know about death?"

Altered

Only Breathing

Life Sentence

I Will Live, Until

If I Must

Fleeting Subsistence

Visions

Tomorrow

ALTERED

"Make your bed
You lie in it..."
I never asked for
Nor wanted this bed –
This white, colorless
Sterile steel contraption...
Void of warmth

It moves
Contours to the shape I want
Lays me down
Sits me up
But, won't release me
To the world
To the outdoors...
To the freshness
Of a serene summer breeze

Here I lay
Feeling trapped
Without any straps
Restrained by the colorless sheets
Wires running in and out
Of my torso
Lights blinking
Sometimes noises blast
Only to warn

Floor to ceiling curtains
Splitting
Dividing - not only the room
But separating me from
The freedom of activity...
Motion, movement

Dee Freeman

The lack of color of this room
Has altered my intellect
I feel

So as I thinketh
So I am, I think
Colorless
Weightless
Motionless
Listless
Semi lifeless

Changing, shifting, transforming –
Slowly
Entering a different mindset
Somehow
Altered

ONLY BREATHING

For years I've lived a closed existence
Not knowing how to live life to it's fullest.
Living a hollow, empty way of life...
A shallow, purposeless life...
In total fear of really living.

Afraid to open up,
Afraid only pain would surface;
Afraid to be me;
Unable to loosen the strings of my heart;
So, I could experience feelings
Of joy, love, ecstasy.

Afraid the pain would bury me deeper
Into my morbid shell.
I cannot open to newness.
I cannot unleash my pent up anxiety.
I cannot soar to new heights.

I cannot awaken the seed of my soul,
By forcing warmed oxygen into my being;
Or trying to blossom to bear fruits
Of brightness and love while suffocating.

I'm thus caught up in lifeless living.
This redundant, unchallenged,
Numb existence which races
Closer and closer to breathlessness.

Dee Freeman

When the hand of life is dealt out
And your cards can't win as the bet is made
Pull from the deck a second chance
You're capable of
Drawing that prized Ace of Spade!!!!

Dee Freeman,
Poet, Author,
Producer, Speaker, Literary Advocate
May, 2006

LIFE SENTENCE

Diagnosed with pulmonary hypertension in the year 2001;
    A life sentence of numbered days for me had begun.
Told by a doctor, I had only three- a maximum of 5 years to live.
    Yet, my Creator said differently,
For numbered days are not man's to give.

The incurable illness was cold and vicious;
    Zapping all energy as it took hold.
I traveled a tumultuous slow road downhill
    Until an inner power took control.

An intravenous tube and pump (Buddy),
    Pushes 24/7 to strengthen and keep me alive.
Yet, God works in mysterious ways-with the doctors,
    They united and have restored my pride.

The life sentence of numbered days I got just five years ago,
    Mean nothing to the Benevolent Power I personally know.
This illness invaded, threatened and racked my being with pain.
    Yet, I'm in the hands of an Omnipotent Master and in Him I'm maintained.

I will not worry; nor let this sentence cause anxiety,
    Discontent or strife.
I now cherish my blessed existence
    And accept this faulty sentence for life.

"In the long run, we shape our lives, and we shape ourselves. The process never ends until we die. And the choices we make are ultimately our own responsibility."

-Eleanor Roosevelt

I WILL LIVE, UNTIL

I will not die until I have lived.
I will not bow to death's audacity;
For I choose to occupy my days
As ordered by my creator,
To remain focused-keeping my
Eye on the prize.

I will not die until I have lived.
I won't yield to the cold hands of death
Until, I have provided purpose and implanted
Passion into the lives of my heirs…leaving
A legacy not soon forgotten.

I will not die until I have lived.
I wont' surrender to mortality's grasp.
I choose boldness and self assurance.
I extend unconditional love…flowing
Like a forceful Water Fall, rushing to ultimately
Blend swiftly, yet smoothly into the
Mighty river…of life.

I choose authenticity of self…to be me!
Free, unchained, unrestrained;
To breathe,
      To live,
To give
      And give.

For I will not die until I have lived.
I will not die until my feebleness can no longer
Ward off death's entrapment-
Death's grip.
Then I must reluctantly and begrudgingly succumb…
Fulfilled…
Because I have lived.

"In all true love there is the love of the Infinite in the person or thing we love."

> Juan Mascaro (?-1987). Introduction
> To Bhagavad Gita (th cent. B.C.)
> 1962

IF I MUST

Die if I must…
Before I do, let me bask in your love
So I'll have something to which I can compare
My life here on earth
Yes…so I'll be reminded of bliss
And drink on the eternity of your sweet kiss

Die if I must…
Before I go, let me smother you with adoration
Soft and gentle tenderness
Like the feel of Cotton Candy dissolving on my tongue
So you may feel and know the sweetness
The passion, the depth
The intensity of my love

Die if I must…
Before I leave you…rise up, come my love
Take wing and fly into my open arms
You've stroked and caressed my soul
Ever so gently
Ever so faintly, like the perch
Of a butterfly onto a delicate daffodil
Your imprint here is however, as deep as a
Volcanoes' Crater
Where the ash bubbles hot with passion like
The spurt of lava that fizzles
And spills slowly down the slopes

Die if I must…
But as I leave this realm,
Shedding this flesh-not my love…
Moving on to another…
The heavens will summon your presence to
Satisfy this ache in my heart
I vow, my love will forever beckon to you
And yield unto you
A time without end of
Sincere undying love

Dee Freeman

"Life is no brief candle to me. It is a sort of splendid torch which I have got hold of for the moment, and I want to make it burn as brightly as possible before handing it on to future generations."

-George Bernard Shaw

FLEETING SUBSISTENCE

Quiet, veiled

Fleeting, transient

Temporary, illusive

Probing, questioning

Igniting into manifestation

Impulsive moments root in the deepest heart chamber
Sprout as threads guided by an unseen hand
Weaving through the fabric of my being

A flicker illuminates embroidery in
My tapestry of life's savoir faire

The discernible needlework subsists for one brief moment
Igniting and glowing with sparks of life
Love and mortality
Constructing flares of creativity
That shine
Flickering only fleetingly
Then, dim
Fade and lessen to oblivion

We are but a momentary twinkle
In this great expanse of time

"The vision we now require is nothing short of a new covenant. At root, we need to return to our spiritual identity as the children of God."

        Jim Wallis (1948-). The soul of Politics:

        A Practical and Prophetic Vision for Change, 3, 1994

VISIONS

I Envision A Place
Where All People
Therein Are Free.

I Envision A World
Of Peace
And That Is
Where I Want To Be.

I Envision A Place
Where Justice Is Not Blind;
A Place Where
Lots Of Love Abide.

I Envision A Wonderful
Heavenly Home, So Peaceful;
That's Where I
Wish To Eternally Reside.

"Drop the question what tomorrow may bring, and count as profit every day that fate allows you."

-Horace

TOMORROW

Draw near
Slowly

Stand close and weep
Quietly

Remember me
Kindly…
As you reminisce on the past

Gaze down on my face
That no longer smiles
Touch my hand
That once cradled
You with warmness
And soothed with gentle
Affection

Look upon me
Today

Hold my memory
Forever

Take heed and prepare
As I am
Today
So shall you be
Tomorrow

POETRY SHE WROTE II: REFLECTIONS OF THE HEART

To God Be The Glory For The Things He Has Done. The Lord truly has done great things through Delores , (Dee) in this magnificent collection of poems. Poetry She Wrote II: Reflections of The Heart gives those who read the words and those who hear the words, a tremendous power of faith, hope, and love.

The poems of 'Aspirations' give us permission to "want"…to want the better, to want a nicer world, to want to share a blessing. Whereas, all too often, our past may tell us "wanting" is in vain. In addition to want, we are encouraged to 'Seize The Moment', 'Never To Tire', and to 'Make A Difference'. Dee's words add new meaning to tradition as she brings to life her thoughts, ideas, charm and passion to create her own message to the world.

The poems on "Searching" allow us to probe, make inquiries and examine ourselves. We are challenged by Dee to ask and perhaps to even answer the questions; who are we; why are we here and what is our purpose? She challenges us to raise our awareness, gather our voices, and loosen our minds, to educate and elevate ourselves and to think out of the "box". I am deeply touched by her gift of the written and spoken word. These are her own expressions of life in a world filled with so much uncertainty and many trials and tribulations.

Dee demonstrates "A Passion for Poetry". Her dedication to humankind can be seen deeply in the poem titled "My Life's Passion" that speaks to: Energize, stimulate, intensify, kindle, accelerate, alleviate and provide. Looking back over the years we have known each other, I can see 'Passion' is what Dee truly has always demonstrated throughout all of her collections of poems.

What insight. "Still Me" could not be made any plainer in this section on "Reality". This is a masterpiece…A work of art. So genuine, so rich in thought, and so well blended in mind, body, and soul. Just imagine with me, a little kinky haired girl, who moves through life's journey with a key stroke and a pen from knowing nothing about the world, to a star of a woman who can explore the universe through her poetry and declare "Still Me".

I am grateful that Dee devoted a section of her book to " Real Love" for we know in John 3: 16 that the bible states , For God so loved the world that he gave his only begotten son that who so ever believeth in him shall have everlasting life. Dee's words on " Love" are best described in her poem "Touching Lives". This is our <u>mission</u>. God loves us so that we may love others.

Weaving it all together, " Aspirations, Searching, Passion, Reality, Real Love, and Closing Stages"; Dee's book of poetry like our lives, must close. In this section " Closing Stages" Dee delivers an in creditable ending with her last poem " Tomorrow" Draw Near Slowly, Stand Close and weep, Quietly Remember me Kindly, as you reminisce on the past. We the class of 1964 will always remember " Our Role Model". How can we forget…we cannot! Delores, Class of 1964, Valedictorian, Richard B. Harrison High School, Blytheville, Arkansas. Superb work Dee. A renewing of my soul.

Thank you Dee for your many gifts of love through your work of poetry. I am privileged and grateful to share this Afterword on " Poetry She Wrote II: Reflections of The Heart. May you always be Blessed, as you have Blessed so many others and me through your expression of poetry and love.

With Love
Your Friend and Classmate
Geraldine Smothers, MPA, RHIA, CSL, CPHQ
    President and CEO
    Professional Dynamic Network, Inc.
    The Jordan Evans Institute.
Temp Staffing for healthcare - Specializing in Health Information Management (Medical Records)

AFFIRMATIONS FOR SELF AWARENESS:

I offer my hands, to work diligently in the service to mankind.
I offer my mind, to think thoughts of intelligence amid brilliant ideas of resourcefulness.
I offer my eyes, to shine brightly, while transmiting radiant reflections of my soul.
I offer my feet, to walk in the path of righteouness so I may become whole.
I offer my heart, to love my fellowman purely and unconditionally.
I offer my words…to you today. Take them, absorb, digest and assimilate them. They are yours to do as you will.

I wish you to live life to it's fullest. I'm striving to do so, even as I write this. Life is not an easy journey-not at all. You must take some hits, some misses, some heartaches and many falls. The ultimate goal is to always get up; stronger than before you fell; learning, using and sharing each of life's lessons.

I truly believe one can learn and grow a little each single day our Creator allows us breath. This belief has sustained me through many difficult times; it continues to uplift my spirit when I feel down.

I hope you will utilize the following pages to express some thoughts or emotions that will assist you in your personal growth, mental development and physical conditioning.

May peace, joy and love, follow you all the days of your life.

"The journey is not yours; it's the Lord's."

The following are journaling pages for today's woman to reflect on her life, her relationships, her weaknesses, her goals and her triumphs.

AFFIRMATIONS
FOR SELF AWARENESS:
Though I struggle desperately to be more Christlike; my human frailties reduce me in spite
You always have choice!

AFFIRMATIONS
FOR SELF AWARENESS:
"No man is an island"
I cannot journey through life alone
I need support, I need to support
Until I journey home
Determine to go the distance!

AFFIRMATIONS
FOR SELF AWARENESS:
Holy Spirit,
Let me be humble and meek
With your Grace within
Allow me to rise above myself
The world is yours for the asking!

AFFIRMATIONS
FOR SELF AWARENESS:
I am preciously amd divinely made
I will therefore live a treasured and consecrated life with You as
my maker, my guide, my joy
and my Savior
He will always make a way!

AFFIRMATIONS
FOR SELF AWARENESS:
Temptation is all around
Therefore, I must envelope myself with
Your holiness, Lord
Love is the answer!

AFFIRMATIONS
FOR SELF AWARENESS:
Sometimes, loving yourself ain't easy
Yet, you must begin this journey
In order to reach a destination
Aim High!

AFFIRMATIONS
FOR SELF AWARENESS:
I offer my hands,
To work diligently
I offer my mind,
To think righteously
I offer my heart,
To love unconditionally
A living sacrifice!

AFFIRMATIONS
FOR SELF AWARENESS:
As I search within;
I ponder the questions:
What can I give?
How is it I should live?
Live ABUNDANTLY!

AFFIRMATIONS
FOR SELF AWARENESS:
Let me shine my light;
Do my part...
Let me share true love
From a pure and caring heart!
Love self foremost, yet exemplify humility!

AFFIRMATIONS
FOR SELF AWARENESS:
From our opening scene, until the final act;
Our appearance on life's stage
Must be of humility and humanity;
Sharing the spotlight, yet promoting Yourself-
The divine Star!!
As you act; so you are!

POETRY SHE WROTE II: REFLECTIONS OF THE HEART

By Dee Freeman
Lansing, Michigan 48917
517 321-3122
deekfreeman@yahoo.com
WWW. deepoette.com

Pen name -	Dee Freeman
Book size	6X9
ISBN	XXX- e-book; XXX- paperback
Binding	Paper back,145 $_+$ pages
Publishing date	2006
Audience	Poetry and prose lovers
Availability	2006

ABOUT BOOK

This collection of poetry, "Poetry She Wrote II: Reflections of The Heart", expresses the need and desire for every entity to know and believe in him/her self, and know there is an Omnipotent power that maintains every destiny and fate. This all powerful presence can be felt by anyone with ability to tune in to oneself-finding self love. Dee Freeman feels many of us have been searching for answers since the beginning of time. Even though we continue the quest, we have yet to find a universal answer that touches on real truth capable of squelching our inquisitiveness. We have yet to find a simple answer that will satisfy this need to unveil the real mystery of life.

This poetry addresses aspects of life from a woman's point of view, as she journeys and searches through every nook and cranny on earth, then scans the heavens for truth, answers and awareness.

This central theme reinforces the fact that people have a strong faith and are determined to continue their search until they no longer breathe. There are miles to be traveled before reaching the ultimate plateau of awareness and contentment. Dee wishes to help in this conquest with these diverse literary expressions. This collection reveals a number of experiences she has personally encountered while traveling this journey.

These poems and prose convey a message, express sentiment, pose unanswered questions, inspire determination, encourage love and togetherness, promote pride, open the emotional window to the heart and invoke inspirational healing. Their clarity and lucidity motivate as they foster: self-esteem, self-confidence, self-love, self-awareness, healing and a sense of well-being.

This collection provides the reader with ample time to read, ponder, absorb and experience a spectrum of emotions – enjoying the message and feeling the gentle touch to the soul. This, like her previous books of poetry, is of great benefit to all-touching, healing, awakening, soothing. The poems reverberate the desire and longing each soul demonstrates in order to know the real meaning of life, while emphasizing how each person has a duty to live, love and leave a legacy. Her plea for universal love-total and unconditional, continues. Her desire is that everyone will enjoy the journey of life-with all its' mysteries-from beginning to end!!

How to Order Autographed copy!!!

Dee Freeman welcomes your direct orders

Discounts available to wholesalers and booksellers

Orders from Individuals

Qty:	Title:	Price Amt.

Subtotal..................$_____

Postage & Handling..........$_____

Total amt. enclosed....$_____

(Add $2.50 for the first 1 or 2 copies
and $1.00 for each additional copy)

Do not send cash. Write your check or money order to:
and mail to:

Dee Freeman
1127 Alexandria Dr.
Lansing, MI 48917

Please allow two weeks for delivery

Orders from Individuals:

Name:_____

Address:_____

City,State,Zipcode:_____

MORE BOOKS BY DEE FREEMAN

Where to get them!!
The Way Station,
Schuler's Book Store,
AuthorHouse.com, Amazon.com,
Barnes & Noble
www.deepoette.com
and deekfreeman@yahoo.com

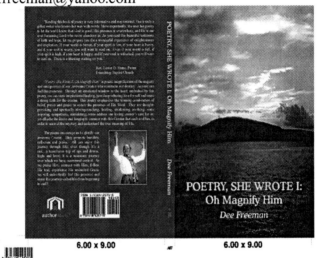

POETRY SHE WROTE II: REFLECTIONS OF THE HEART

ABOUT AUTHOR

Delores , (Dee) is excited about life. She continues to be motivated-striving for excellence. A compelling and dynamically gifted poet and author; producer and host; mother and grandmother; friend and Christian; wife and companion to her loving husband, Atty. Myron Freeman, Sr., Dee is always expanding and reaching for higher achievements. She is using her love, skills and creativity to help readers enjoy expressions and rhythmic rhyme. She left the south to follow an extremely elusive dream, which finally, she's living and enjoying-her passion-writing. Almost everyone is talking about Freeman's well received books "Oceans of Love: To Us From Us" and Poetry She Wrote I: Oh, Magnify Him". Both have been placed in the school system and libraries around town. Her poems appear in magazines, anthologies and news papers and many have been recognized with awards for their inspirational, motivational and reality check messages.

Freeman looks forward to expanding her Poetree-N-Motion TV program which attracts a wide and diverse audience. Producing and hosting this show not only showcases her poetic prowess and creative abilities, she shares information of community events, history tidbits, book reviews and has guests with current community issues. She encourages other artists to come spread their artistic and creative wings as they too, soar to new heights. The show airs in Lansing on Comcast channel 16 -Thursday @ 3:30PM; East Lansing channel 30 WELM on Tuesday @ 7:00PM and daily in Detroit, Comcast channel 68.

Multi-talented, she's hoping to have musical lyrics recorded in the near future. Her dream of having a number one seller is closing in, as she has completed her first fiction novel-a project in conjunction with a movie producer. This novel- "Wild, Untamed Michigan: The Way It Was" is scheduled to hit the stores in 2006, with her youth poetry book, "To Heir Is To Love" following closely. These are fabulous gifts for any book lover. Her books "Oceans of Love: To Us From Us" and "Poetry, She Wrote I: Oh Magnify Him", as well as this one-"PSW II", are available at The Way Station, Schuler's Book Store, AuthorHouse.com, Amazon.com, www.deepoette.com, de_poette@hotmail.com and Barnes & Noble.

An alumnus of Northwood University of Midland and former Financial Analyst for General Motors, Freeman resides in Lansing, Michigan with her husband. She is grateful to her spouse and their grandson-Giovanni-who inspires many pieces with today's youths in mind. She is proud of her three adult children, one of whom has attained stardom as an actor on Broadway and extremely thankful to supporters of her show and poetry. She appreciates the opportunity to share her work and wants her readers to (BBB) BE BOUNTIFULLY BLESSED and know, they already are who they wish to be. She maintains, "The challenge is to open up to become the new you that is within you."

Reach Freeman via e-mail— deekfreeman@yahoo.com or de_poette@hotmail.com or website www.deepoette.com.

Printed in the United States
67352LVS00004B/349-375